The Fish Lizard of Lyme

In this story we are told
of someone worth their weight in gold.
So look inside (it won't take ages)
just *who* is hiding in these pages?

The Fish Lizard of Lyme

(a little tale that's told in rhyme)

by

Carolyn King

Roving Press
Step-Up Books

© 2013 Carolyn King

Published by Roving Press Ltd under the imprint 'Step-Up Books'
4 Southover Cottages, Frampton, Dorset, DT2 9NQ, UK
Tel: +44 (0)1300 321531
www.rovingpress.co.uk

Distributed by Legassick Studio
'Seagulls' 21 Wessiters, Seaton, Devon EX12 2PW
Email: p.clayton877@btinternet.com
Tel: +44 (0)1297 23115
www.westcountryartists.com

All rights reserved. No part of this publication may be reproduced, stored in a retrieval system or transmitted, in any form or by any means, electronic, mechanical, photocopying or otherwise, without the prior permission of the publisher.

First published 2013 by Roving Press Ltd

ISBN: 978-1-906651-213 Hard back
ISBN: 978-1-906651-206 Soft back

British Library Cataloguing in Publication Data
A catalogue record for this book is available from the British Library

Set by Beamreach (www.beamreachuk.co.uk)
Printed and bound by Henry Ling Ltd, at the Dorset Press, Dorchester DT1 1HD

With special thanks to the Lyme Regis ArtsFest Team and Lyme Regis Museum.

This book has been inspired by the palaeontologist Mary Anning, who in 1811, together with her younger brother, discovered the first Ichthyosaur on Lyme beach.

It has been produced as part of **re: collection**, a joint project between Lyme Regis ArtsFest and Lyme Regis Museum supported using public funding by the National Lottery through Arts Council England.

For
Suzanne and Philip
with love

Introduction

Welcome, welcome one and all
It's great to see you big or small.
I hope you've come to hear my tale
About a creature (like a whale).

When I was little (just like you)
I found a creature no one knew,
Hiding almost out of reach
In the cliffs above the beach.

And I worked hard to set him free
So he could talk to you and me.
But before I tell you of his name
I'd like to tell you *why* he came
Across the distant past to Lyme,
Where we can find him if we've time!

L̲ong, long ago when the Earth was young
The Land and the Sea could never agree
On whom was the most important of all.

(But pride they say goes before a fall
And as this tale will soon now tell,
a lot of other things as well!)

"I've got Dinosaurs big and bold!"
was the story the Land then told.
"With great big teeth and great big feet
To tread your waves and eat and eat!"

"Well," said the Sea who swelled with pride,
"I have bigger things inside;
I have fish who leap and dive
And gobble those of twice their size!"

On they argued night and day
But neither one would 'ere give way.
The Land shot fire 10 miles high
and singed the birdies in the sky;

The Sea dumped weed and rubbish too,
which made the beach all Stinky Poo!

So Rain was sent to spoil their play
(just like it often does today).

Then both the Sun and Moon decided (as over Earth they both presided)
That Moon would rule the *Sea* by night and Sun would give the *Land* its light.
(And birds who could both swim and fly would be dealt with by and by.)

Long ages passed and things were fair (until each forgot they had to share).
But soon the Sea began to grow as sunshine melted Ice and Snow
And fishes swam now far and wide, where others had no place to hide.

7

The Moon then had a cunning plan.

"I'll help the Sea all I can and that will give me much more space
To see my '*beauti-fully*' face."

"I'll pull the Sea with all my might
a little higher night by night
and whilst the Land is fast asleep
he will not notice water creep
along his shores (and up his rivers);
I'll send him fish to make him shiver!"

So when the tide was at its height
it flooded everything in sight.

In raced creatures, all shapes and sizes eager to explore.
Some evolved and called it home,
Some did not and felt alone.

And all the while
the Moon did spread across the Sea and smile.

And all the while the Sun did wait upon
this fact and deliberate what to do.

The Land was small, too small to bear
all the creatures living there.
So the Sun, now bold and bright,
shone more (as if to make amends)
And soon the Seas began to fall,
evaporate like magic (and the fish were penned).

Rivers, clogged with reeds and bogs
no fish could ever navigate, dried up.

Now caught between the two, those creatures who could swim and run
(My friend was one) kept cool by night,
Tried to follow rivers to their source;
Whilst others stayed behind to wallow in the swampy mud
Got stuck, of course
(For us to find).

The skies were blue, the Sun was hot, the hills were very steep.
My friend was tired but plodded on with very painful feet.
A most miserable of places
With laughing monkey faces,
He wished he'd never come.

My friend turned back from mountain streams,
His head was full of nasty dreams,
Then something bit his bum!

"Oh, this for me is not the way.
I must decide to catch the tide to live another day."

So right at the water's edge now,
A tear, a shrug, a sigh
To his fellow creatures on the swamp
He waved a last goodbye.

His nice warm rock was cosy,
But soon the night would come
And beasties from the forest
Would eat them, one by one!

He wriggled his toes in the twilight
He spread his fingers wide.
He shut his eyes and leapt
He made his 'historic' dive!

On and on he swam,
　Searching for that special place

(Somewhere he'd be nice and safe).

And through the ages of the world
He began to change.

He struggled quite a bit poor chap
Unsure of what to use his fingers for.
And then his toes began to web
And his nose got longer.

He grew a fin, became quite slim,
And now he could outrun the monsters of the deep.

Until at last one afternoon he found a place to sleep.

At first the people ran away.

But soon he found a friend

And this is where our tale began
And this is where it ends.

Now fossil hunters from far and wide
Come seek him on a falling tide.
They hear how he was brave and bold
(And how he's worth his weight in gold).

He's whom I made this poem for and his name is

Ichthyosaur!